BOA
EDITIONS
LIMITED

Each in His Season

Poems by
W. D. Snodgrass

BOA Editions, Ltd. Brockport, NY 1993

LC #: 92–73594
ISBN: 0–918526–98–1 Cloth
ISBN: 0–918526–99–X Paper

First Edition
2 3 4 5 6 7 8 9 0

The publication of books by BOA Editions, Ltd.,
is made possible with the assistance of grants from
the Literature Program of the New York State Council on the Arts
and the Literature Program of the National Endowment for the Arts,
as well as from the Lannan Foundation and the Lila Wallace – Reader's Digest
Literary Publishers Marketing Development Program.

Cover Design: Daphne Poulin
Typesetting: Foerster FineLines, York Beach, ME
Manufacturing: McNaughton & Gunn, Lithographers
BOA Logo: Mirko

BOA Editions, Ltd.
A. Poulin, Jr., President
92 Park Avenue
Brockport, NY 14420

CONTENTS

V. IN FLOWER

for Kathy

all the time

I

Birds Caught, Birds Flying

Anniversary Verses
for My Oldest Wife

I vowed and vowed again
I'd marry me no more;
I hadn't met you then.
I reswear all I swore.

Too young to have known better,
You laid down, side by side,
Our differences together:
Your has-been; my child bride.

Through ten years you've endured
Me older than all others;
Since aging hasn't cured
Your tastes, stay thou my druthers.

Only our second night
We ended up at last;
This new dog's learned the right
Old dame can fix you fast.

As a Child, Sleepless

The possum under the owl's claw,
The wet fawn huddled in the grass,
The soldier, hurt, in his lost trench
Clench the eyelid, clutch the breath
Till scavengers, till *coup de grâce*,
Death and the lurking terror pass.

Vice tight each muscle lest the pent
Tendon spasm, twitch; preserve
All rigor, silence, so the blood
Thuds slower, fainter through the vein
Till the chilled skin gives off no scent;
Drain all least current from the nerve.

Clamp the arm tight against the head
To hush that whisper in the nose,
The click if lips slip open. Cover
Over this face and form; disguise
Whose body's lying on the bed,
Eyes that stare still too wide to close.

THE GIRL OUTSIDE YOUR WINDOW

                    doesn't know
she doesn't know you
                    doesn't notice
you've noticed her,
                    does not care
what you care about, won't
care if you don't care.
She shifts the square brown
sack
            for herself
to her left arm, wraps
her torn school jacket
tight around her
            not for you
thin chest and turns away
to watch these dingy cars
lined up at trackside, idling,
waiting for your train
            for you
to pass.
                    Once you get
gone, this slim girl
            for herself
will move on, on her
errand, the drab cars
go their own way,
            their own ways;
the rundown bar, these gray
frame buildings, families
in each one of these houses
go on being, happening, all
                    day every day;
lights come on, go off
            not for you
each night, each morning;
            no part of this

switched on
    for you
        switched off
once you get gone.
           Your train
jolts, recoils. Outside,
cars edge up, she shifts weight,
the conductor calling, "Board!"
You surge ahead, as your train's
door clangs your car closed
like a ship inside a bottle.
The railway whistle wails
out across town, the river
valley, up the cliffsides
toward the horizon as you hurl
down rails laid down toward nothing
she knows, nothing she
        could care about:
your music lesson in the city,
    Is she neglected, beaten?
lunch, then, at your father's club
with clients,
        Chilled or hungering?
        not to mention
the unmentionable lady friend.
      Sleepless, nights, in bed?
        The train's long howl,
your foolish questions hang
unanswered in this closed air
like a note inside a bottle,
some message scrawled out,
desperate, in a foreign hand.

THE SEALCHIE'S SON

> *"It shall come to pass on a summer's day*
> *When the sun shines hot on every stone*
> *That I shall take my little young son*
> *And teach him how to swim the foam."*
> — The Great Sealchie of Sule Skerry

Grizzled old stranger. What did he
Want with us? What right had he
Nosing out around our fencerows? —
Him in his salt's old leather gear,
Greasy, rough, one eye cocked like he'd
Known us somewhere, like he'd owned us.

Even the housedogs howled at him.
Then when my mother unlatched our gate
And he shambled in across our doorsill,
They tucked their tails in and slunk off;
Not one of them came out in sight
The whole two days that he stayed here.

Those two — what did they say together?
I heard his harsh, outlander's voice
Sounding our kitchen but could not
Fathom out so much even as one word.
My heart went clammy in my chest.
I wanted to crawl in underneath the dogs.

That hot, wide, yellowy stare — it
Changed things anywhere it lighted.
He looked at them; they went strange.
When he fixed his hard claw here on
My sleeve, trying to talk to me . . .
My arm aches cold, still, with that touch.

Now all he saw, all's gone alien.
The chairs are awkward, wrong.
I pace the kitchen, sit; I pace again.
Nothing there in my own house remains
That will still have me. I choke down
Meals, turn back outside to the fields.

What strain's got into me, contrary,
Making the whole of it so restless?
I turn a stranger to my own bed;
I pitch, toss; sleep will not take me in.
Or I wake up and can't quite recall
What dreams battered and consoled me.

Some nights, a few, I wake to find
Myself on the sea beach, here. Here
I rest for long hours, hearing
The unshamed crying of the gulls,
Or watch the old surf stroke the sand
At my feet, smooth, murmuring its calm.

In broad day, I sit looking out
Over slate waves to those sun-gathering
Stones where the great seals loll,
Nuzzling the soft flanks of their mates,
Nuzzling their fat cubs, warm against
Each other in the chill wash of the sea.

VENUS AND THE LUTE PLAYER

My nails, light, on these strings.

On roadside wires, far off, shy kestrels
Touch down. Clasped in their talons,
All tidings hum like insects: the death
Of someone dearly loved, the death of love,
Aspirations of the young, the lies, the sighs
Of businessmen and lovers. They ride
Impulses, pounding, that go to drive iron
Foundries, light our highways, houses,
And might warm our lives. Those cables,
To the light wind's testing, whisper;
The birds wait . . .

In pine woods, silent, a hunter takes sight,
Arches the bowstring to his cheek, his ear,
And waits. The ten-point buck
Stands listening, his great flank quivering
Through whose deep circuitry and conduits flow
The slow tides, the unaging currents
That could feed a family all winter
Or could spring free, still, regain the herd
To stand guard on its kind, strong against
Recognizance. Ears twitch. That fletched
Annunciation, the string's song waits . . .

These fingers, just so, weigh and balance
Seeds that must go broadcast through the air,
Then fall, patterned, earthward where they rise
Like detonations on the radar's screen,
That draw upon some hoard of past deaths
Depositing our ground to lift a porch's
Morning glories tangled in their lattices,
As the heart's waves, blue, on monitor,
Or whole notes, *cantus firmus*, implicit

In the tablature — as seeds I lift in hand
To call down songbirds from the sky . . .

Or, soon enough, these fingers pass
Across your belly where . . .

And we begin the song.

LOVE LAMP

There's our candle, on the bedstand still,
That served, warm nights, for lovelight
And the rays of its glass panels played
On our entangled legs and shoulders
Like some sailor's red and blue tattoos
Or as cathedral stained glass altars
Congregated flesh to things less
Carnal, tinged by its enfolding glow.

What could that frail lamp seem
To prowlers outside — the fox, say, the owl,
Or to some smaller creature, shrieking,
Pierced in the clutch of tooth and claw
That interrupted love's enactments?
Our glancing flashlight, though, showed
Only scattered grey fur, some broken
Feathers, bloodstained, on the lawn.

Scuttling back to bed, a little
Chilled from the wet grass, we scratched
A match restoring our small gleam
To see there, sinking in soft wax,
The wings and swimming dark limbs
Of that moth — still there, hardened
By the years like amber. While I remember
The scathing fire-points of his eyes.

Birds Caught, Birds Flying

I handed you, for you to hold —
as a surgeon some live tissue —
the chickadee that had slipped through
our open window, then went
fluttering, blundering around
our walls. While we processioned
room to room with it, you felt
it pulsing, shivering against
that tender cage of fingers. Outside,
you stroked its back once, took
your hand away; upraised there
on the altar of your palm, it sat
still, blinking, till it knew it
had survived, and flew away.

Two years after you left, I came
back to this locked house; starlings
had been down the chimney. They must
have circuited, dark ghosts, the cold
abandoned rooms, dodged among
our furnishings, gone battering
against the lightning flash of panes
as a neurotic goes on battering
at habits he can't break.
Then died down. I found
one drowned in the toilet, one
behind the bed — mere white bones
wreathed by their own feathers.
Mice or maggots took all else.

In the marketplace at San Miguel
once, I bought a sparrow hawk
that fainted at my touch. Kept
only overnight, those bright wings
flashed toward the morning's jacarandas.
Now, hummingbirds that snare themselves

high in our garage's dormer,
chickadees that knock themselves
against our windows — they peer
out through our arched fingers like
a transplant between ribs.
We stroke them, once, to life again,
and watch them go on, on their way
again then, when they must be gone.

PRETEXTS

i.

How to be your own liberator, free
From fixed ideas and, to your own self, true?
What liberates the heart like treachery?

How shall the brain shuck off old habits, be
Cleared for new choices, certain what to do?
How can you work your own deliverance, free

Your sight from bias, letting your self see
Your true needs: what the shrewd stay loyal to?
What need commits the heart like treachery

To shed bad debts, dead faiths, love's tyranny?
When every petty friendship claims its due,
How can you be your own true master, free-

Standing, confirmed in your full energy,
Honed in on prey you've hungered to pursue
And guaranteed in heart by treachery?

Seeing the long good faith you've shown to me
Makes me my own foe, would I dare trust you?
How shall a man be his own saviour, free
To satisfy his own heart? Treachery.

ii.

How shall a man aspire toward what he's not —
Faust's hankering after more than man can be?
What shows you who is who, tells what is what

And proves this world as evil as we thought —
Surely its laws couldn't apply to me?
How shall a man accomplish what he's not,

Accede to those high goals you always sought,
Cowed by the timid mob's morality?
What could insinuate who's who and what's what

Like the illicit coin slipped in love's slot
To charge nerves with a willful energy
And so impel a man toward what he's not?

By some old friend's name we affix the spot
That damns us to a new identity,
A new place in *Who's Who* and that is what

Our clasped hands and fine words at his graveplot
Signify: our soul's nativity
That lets a man assume to what he's not.
Who's no longer who: what, though, will be what.

iii.

To learn, at long last, that you've been betrayed —
Can't that explain the rage you'd always known,
Their sour resistance to all plans you made?

Your best friend's cleaned you to the bare walls, laid
Your one love, left you impassed and alone.
The hard-bought knowledge that you've been betrayed —

This Judas kiss fresh on your cheek displayed —
Demands that certain licenses be shown
To you and those propitious plans you'd made.

It's clear you had good cause to be afraid
And had to take precautions on your own.
To know, at long last, that you've been betrayed

To your old enemies should help persuade
You and the world around you to condone
Certain discretionary plans you made:

How you could move in first to slip your blade
Under the ribs, then drive it to the bone.
To learn how, at long last, you've been betrayed
Proves you just, just any plans you made.

iv.

Tell me about the Brotherhood of Man;
From what I've seen inside *this* family,
I'll take an enemy any time I can.

Track this thing back to where it all began:
Eden, that hotbed of fraternity,
Tells me about the Brotherhood of Man.

The shoe in my spokes, ink spilt on my plan
May be a sincere form of flattery;
Give me flat enmity, give me all you can.

We know who wins votes and who'll lead this clan —
Procrustes, champion of equality;
He'll preach us all the Brotherhood of Man,

His great care for the weak, the also-ran —
While eyeing my change, nudging my wife's knee.
Give me an enemy; find the worst you can.

Tell me you're glad you're an American
Or whatnot, true-blue. Turn up the TV;
Hard sell me on the Brotherhood of Man;
I'll take my enemies every time I can.

ELENA CEAUÇESCU'S BED

Making ourselves at home in that broad bed
    Elena left, we slept snug as the mouse
That, burrowing in guest room blankets, fed
    Her brood last winter in our summer house.

What bed, through all our lives long, had we known
    If not the tyrant's? How many had been driven
Homeless and hungering while I had my own
    Bed, my own room? How many have been given

Lives at hard labor while our markets rose
    And we had all we asked for in the lands
Of milk and honey? Where could you find those
    Who hunted, once, that hill where my house stands?

There'll be just one bed, too soon, for us all.
    What empire's hacked out by the meek, the kind?
The lioness kills; the lion feasts; the small
    Bury their noses in what's left behind.

In Memory of Lost Brain Cells

*— on receiving an honorary doctorate
from Allegheny College, 5/19/91.*

Here, at our Academic Festival,
It's right that we survivors should recall

Those lost from our ranks: bold, selfless neurons
Questioned and persecuted past endurance;

Our agents, gatherers of intelligence
Whose networks through benighted continents

Flashed out curt messages of wit and brilliance
Till marked, seized, whisked away, wiped out by millions,

Never to be replaced. Still, those connections
They formed live on in spite of past defections,

In spite of new betrayals, quislings, quitters.
Others fill in, take up where old transmitters

Shut down. Daily we see more territory
Fall prey to new world orders, to *a priori*

Systems or pressure groupies, find more knowledge
Banned by the thought police, see one more college

Sold out to fixed theories, one more liar
Voted to high office, one more supplier

Of comfy truths belaurelled; each night some drunken
Purge wipes out our cells, leaves us with shrunken

Heads, brains laundered, safe but uninstructed,
One more priceless faculty deconstructed.

Still, who would live in any times but these?
These are the days that try men's synapses,

Nights when we learn what axons and dendrites
Through our dark hemispheres switch on the lights.

We veterans of the brain's unCivil War —
I pray thee ask not one man, one cell more —

We few, we happy few must bless our lot.
What difference if our old professors thought

To grant our doctorate "wouldn't be prudent,"
We can still hope to snag one through a student.

You supersnoops and spies, that CIA
Whose postings keep us live and human, stay

True to your codes of cortical responses,
Facts all men need though none believes he wants us.

Though names, dates, facts fall from our memory,
Stand fast: we shall live through this third degree.

Not all nerves fail; hold your cerebral mission;
This happy day shall doctor our condition.

An Envoi, Post-TURP

(After Trans-Urethral Resectioning of the Prostate, men experience retrograde ejaculation, the semen being passed later during urination.)

Farewell, children of my right hand and bliss.
You'll come no more but in bright streams of piss,
Never more turn my bedroom towels stiff,
Whitewash the walls or glisten on the quiff;
Never more swim like salmon or rough Norse
Invaders swarming upstream to the source.
Once, ovaries were ovaries; sperms, sperms.
In nine short months you brought us all to terms
When captive loins were sentenced by your court
To long years, lawyers' fees and child support.
You cared for just one thing — aye, that's the rub:
Each of you, at your Health and Country Club
Timed training laps, did pushups by the pool
Shunning each voice that cried, "Back, back you fools,
We'll all be killed — it's a blow job!" You hurled
Yourselves, bluff hardy semen, on the world
Like Noah's load that crested with the Flood
To populate the land and stand at stud.
Ink of my pen, you words spent 'εν 'αρχῇ,
This writer, knowing all he's cast away,
Knowing your creamy genes and DNA
Encodes our texts, pirates and then reprints us, says,
"Good night, bad cess to you, sweet prince and princesses."

A Teen-Ager

The high-priced jeans, the new car — she got what
She wanted; she'd been taught to want a lot.
To her girl friend in back, she talked about
Which of her friends shacked up with which. I thought,
"That must be for my benefit. No doubt
She's younger than my daughter. Still, why not?
A glorious redhead. One helps ladies out."

Taking a cigarette, she had to switch
Hands on the wheel to pick a kitchen match
Out of her dungaree shirtpocket which
Seemed quite well filled. Then she reached down to scratch
Fire off those tiny steel teeth that meet, match
And catch closed where her trouserfly's dark patch
Curves under, brightly glittering in her crotch.

I'd seen truck drivers do that. The flames caught;
She lit and sucked in smoke. That's when I got
Snatched back down to facts; I knew why not.
She'd been so spoiled, groomed, fairy-story rich,
She thought hard talk and hard times could be bought
Like poor people's clothes to disguise your niche
In life. Why add my barrel to her notch?

AN OLD FLAME

Some ten years later she still writes,
"My dearest lover" — she, who strove
Mightily fanning up my nights
To a slow burn; who, while I drove

Six hundred miles out of my way
So she could drop in on her ex,
Kvetched at our meals, the rough highway,
My car, my driving, morals; next,

She expatiated on his gorgeous
Ass, high-priced gifts and the delightful
Foreplay that once fueled weeklong orgies.
Too tired, at our motel come nightfall,

She turned her back and snored. Some, lest
Love prove too absolute, too pristine,
Can't sleep till they've fouled their nest
Or drunk the bathwater they've pissed in.

A CURSE

— against A. H.,
who does not make instruments.

You drove off with the applewood
From that great, bounteous tree that stood
Lightning-battered and storm-tortured
Half a century in our orchard
And whose trunk, 20 feet tall, grew
Hard, dark-toned and 2 feet through
Then, seasoning for 10 years, had lain
Waiting a purpose worth its grain;
You took, besides, our walnut, spruce
And cherry boards for your own use
And warm ivory we'd soaked loose
From piano keys. Grave as a goose,
You gave your promise to produce
An instrument, made an excuse
Instead, then sure as self-abuse,
One more excuse, one more, one yet
Till we both knew that's all we'd get.

Now, if you sell that harpsichord
May the straightgrained spruce of its soundboard,
Warping and twisting, wrench apart
So irritable buzzings start
To breed inside that lengthening crack
And pins slip — not enough to slack
Strings though the true pitch won't quite hold.
There, where you signed your name in gold
May random checking split and etch it
Straight through the words, *A. H. Me Fecit.*

Or if you keep it as your own,
May it ring with a strong, clean tone
At times. But when in public may

Jacks swell and jam so that you play
Garbles of chord and melodies
Gapped like decaying teeth or cheese.
May felts fail so each error lingers
Long in the ear and may your fingers
Slip off the ivory, slick as wax,
So you play always in the cracks
Between keys that go limp or stick
Tearing your nail down to the quick.

May all you set your hand to, buckle,
Breaking your finger at the knuckle
Which, aging, aching, goes rheumatic,
Turns your recorder holes asthmatic,
Your fiddle feeble and your squeeze
Box troubled by a sleazy wheeze.
May your drum rhythms stumble and alter
So that the dancers halt, start, falter
And when you lift your voice, may it wobble
As if you'd told things not quite probable.

May far-flung audiences recognize
Just what you are. And may the wise
Try your virginals, guess at their price,
Look long, but think best not to ask it,
Seeing its form's so like a casket
He could go to the boneyard in it
Before you finished him his spinet.

Still, may no formal punishment
Ease your guilt; may each day be spent
Evading lawyers' calls or tax
Inspectors. Falling shy on facts,
On good faith or harmonic rules,
Be fearless around power tools.
Should you pick up some stranger's kit
Or fine wood, switch on your drill bit;
If you should skirt around a law,

Look up once from your band saw;
If you should ever break your faith
May loose hairs wander toward your lathe.

Lastly, may those you trust in break
Their word and for their own sweet sake
Waste your gifts on things to make
Them comfy till the day you die.
Every midnight may you lie
Awake with one who'll scorn and rule
You for a coward and a fool.
That is, I hope you spend your life
Alone — or better, with your wife.

The Ballad of Jesse Helms

(Expletives Deleted and Self-
CENSORED)

Kum, you sheet-heads, KuKu Klucks,
Klandestine Khristers, you dumb
LEGIONS
Of Decency whose burning crux
    Inflames our nether regions,

Acclaim the name of Jesse Helms
Whose moral vision under-
SCORES
That crotches, even oaks' or elms',
    Submit to underdrawers.

Behold this virtuous and reborn soul
Who rose up from his country's corn-
PONE
Crying, "Let us have one sworn goal:
    Life above the porn zone!"

Driving out all that's crude and naughty,
He'll make our world safe for cast-
OFF
And long-forgotten lines of thought we
    Thought we'd heard the last of.

This saintly man from Carolina
Will douche the wet and wild va-
RIETY
Of lusts, then purge us pure as China
    From thought and/or impiety

Soviet censorship's in a slump;
Who'll tell Red Kumrads what to
THINK?
So Helms' Blue Laws give us the jump:
    No one will dare show Pink.

Both Ayatollah and Inquisition
Taught us a missionary
STANCE:
Hold still for our kind of coition
    Or we'll cut off your grants.

Schicklgruber and Djugashvili
Died; men dare speak frank and
PUTRID
Facts. Jesse, firmly but genteelly,
    Will keep all knowledge neutered.

Our last, best hope — though some suspect
He's grown too old to get e-
QUIPPED
For the Grand Campaign that he'll direct
    To keep the engorged world zipped.

Nosing out all that's vile and heinous
He stuck his head in his old
TEXTS
And found this creed: "We must maintain us
    One and one half sex —

"We'll simply order all the arts
To satisfy the same old
RULES
That razor out the juicy parts
    And burn books in our schools.

"We'll jam our message right up front:
Give us no cock and
BULL, IMMORAL
Tales depicting obscene, blunt
Anal events or oral.

"Though evangelists and Senators,
Congressmen who frequent
RESIDENTS,
Commit such acts behind closed doors
And talk filth fit for presidents,

"Now artists claim such rights; they'd share
Powers of committees that we chair
-ISH.
They've asked our aid. That's only fair:
Let them have Aids and perish!"

With chapter, verse and catechism
He proved he's got the juice and
PASSION
To lift us up from lust's abysm,
Whiteshirts joined in a new Fas-
HION.

He'll save souls at a faster rate
With his crusade to master
REALMS
Ennobled since emasculate,
Kept marketable and steered straight
By gunboats from our ship of state
With Jesse at their **HELMS.**

II

The Midnight Carnival

**A Collaboration with the Painter,
DeLoss McGraw**

THE CAPTURE OF MR. SUN

The sun is a lion
 circling his cage,
Caught for you, brought for you
 on this wheeled stage,
Through fixed bars glaring
 his wrath and his rage
Like a pen for the baby
 or bedrails in old age.

The lion is a sunflower
 with a broad gold face,
Its petals outstreaming
 like a mane or the rays
Of that candescent Power
 we all watch pace
Through the gendering heavens
 on its circuit of days.

The flower is tracing
 the sun on its rounds;
The carnival moves through
 its orbit of towns;
The lion's cage rolls
 your streets up and down
Where he pads and we shiver
 at his smile, his frown.

W. D.'s Carnival Friends

What did you see at the carnival?
What did you learn to tell us all?

I saw a pig with a tambourine
Dancing a jig till he spun the scene;

I saw a man with a great cockscomb,
A baby dressed like a cutthroat gnome;

A little girl in a bright pink skirt
Turning her eyes down in the dirt;

A boy with a pair of rabbit ears
Hanging his head at what he hears;

A man so starved out that he's grown
All sticks and joints of dead-white bone;

A clown grown fat as a globe of meat
As if all earth were his own to eat;

I saw a pig with a tambourine;
A Satanical wolf with a snout of green,
His teeth bared, glittering and obscene.
An angel hovered above this scene
Whose eyes were closed and his smile serene.

But where does it lead and what does it mean?
I saw a pig with a tambourine . . .

HOUSE OF HORRORS

Only a dollar, folks, only one
      lowdown devalued dollar for a full
breath-stopping half-hour's agony —
      this one time, every second of your
living, breathing lifetime, climb
      fist over foot and toe past finger up
our light-bright, particolored, unsupported
      ladder through heat-lightninged air
past pure primaries, past the varied
      complementaries and, last, past
all prismatic tints and shades till you attain
      to that high perch there where it teeters
on its circus tight wire — and but no,
      it's not the sun, blind source of colors —
and but yes, this black pavilion tent,
      our elevated pit and black hole
where all light and energies rush in
      and fail; yet, yes, but once inside
and it gets hard to tell it from
      Versailles' vast Hall of Mirrors
where cataclysmic peace broke out;
      as if the polished granite pillars of
burnt Persepolis gave back your face,
      the walls of Altamira your nickname
and secret vices; as if the air
      held all sound waves created
since the first big bang, a sort of
      tape recorder under your best bed or
Quaker meeting in the craphouse —
      welcome, in the end then, to the great
kakangelist's big top and revival
      for the psalm and badspel of our days:
the world is much the way the world
      wants; it's too late for you to change.
It is as if it's just like what it is.

HALL OF MIRRORS

This mirror, fine-spun chromium,
    is buffed so bright
it will set fires for you some
    moonless night.

The next is scoured, filmed, a clouded
    -over mystery
crystal where you can read a shrouded
    face and history.

This shows where you've been, what you've done
    to whom; this, who
's gaining on you. The blanked-out one,
    where you're bound to.

This mirror shows what might have been
    if you'd had means,
love, funds, chances, prominent kin
    or different genes.

This storage mirror holds the past
    as its fixed prize,
past blame, past changing and, at last,
    excuse or lies.

This turns you to a multitude
    of shouting clones;
this shrinks you to a leaf-mite who'd
    lurk under stones;

this turns you to a bulgy sphere;
    this to a pole;
this steals your feet, head, knees, while here,
    this drinks your soul.

The last, the rarest, shows you in
      -side out; your smile,
manner, hair-do, and smooth, warm skin
      are out of style

and sight. Like insects', your bared bones
      support and clothe
you, white as the foundation stones
      of all you loathe.

WIRE WALKER

This elevation's atmosphere's
Thin in your lungs, chill on your ears

And the crowd's prayers, like hot air, rise
In hopes you'll fall before their eyes

Cracking your bones back to their level
Like wrecked kites or some downcast devil;

Soon as they've handed you their laurel,
Thorn or gold crown, there's a choral
Wail of dissent: "Are such heights moral?

"Let's check his feet for the pure slime
We live in; some deep flaw or crime
Drives any anti-social-climb."

They'd have each high muckety-muck,
Poobah, or savior shit-out-of-luck
And shot down — a lame, ruptured duck —

So they applaud my heavy friend as
He steals the net from my stupendous
Finale: Last of the Wallendas.

They cheer the fall of every sparrow.
Mounting my bicycle or wheelbarrow,
I keep strict to the straight and narrow;

This road's shoulders are less than soft.
As waves of their ill feeling waft
Upwards, ill winds buoy me aloft

Where, as hawks draft on thermal currents,
I bank on ill-will: flight insurance
Drawn on my uplift and endurance.

Ambling this bright, unfriendly skyway,
I can't roam one dark lane or byway;
Straight, straight ahead lies my way;
Who needs lane-lines on this lone highway?

HUMAN TORCH

What use gas, coal or alcohol?
I burn a fossil fuel refined
And volatile past all men's thought:
Old losses, wounds, lost loves that fall
Like leaves beneath earth's weight, then brought
Back up — pure heartburn of the mind.

My lady love, trim in her green
Short skirt — my other ball and chain —
Holds up a wooden kitchen match;
As welders set acetylene
Alight by squeeze and spark, she'll scratch
Her lucifer to fire my brain.

My friend, this globe-shaped, saintly George
Like a hose-truck or water-wagon
Fears my best flames. He'd douse and drench
The gimp-legged blacksmith at that forge
Where love and war fused; could well quench
The ancient, quintessential dragon.

The crowd values my flaming tongue
As an expensive power tool
To light cigars or a barbecue;
Some think I should inflame the young
To run riot, or like some voodoo
Priest, spew out rum and holy drool.

I save my breath to set alight
Wine in cut crystal, gems that bedizen
A lady's jugular and snow
White throat, fireflies in woods at night,
The stars' far campfires and the glow
Of morning soft at the horizon.

Tattooed Man

how come i get no say what
    my skin says, chances to write
over, scratch out, explain explain *one*
    prize lamb. seven goats to be paid off
say like if your computer screen or
    the Times Building ran fake newsreels,
blue cartoons **lasciate ogni speranza**
    accursed by my own gift of tongues
with only future tenses i can't
    understand *shall forever be*
just as it has been i am all bass
    ackwards in the mirror MEAN
RAINFALL FOR 736 WILL RISE no man
    need testify against himself; i bear
my wrist's dyed ID number *The Visigoth*
    United Liberation Front will convene
wear my treacheries around my neck,
    chest, biceps: fraternizing with
my own best enemy, myself. am i my
    allusive Pisan cantos, my Nazi
lampshade to read them by Ἐν ἀρχῇ
    ἦν ὁ λόγος no cryptologist
deciphers me ALBERT ELEUTHERIA '03
    LOVES the same as any other but
they add their names. like if i am
    my own Laws' tablets **mene mene**
tekel u-pharsin why does, when
    my lady turns towards my fat worst
friend and smiles *ATTENTION SHOPPERS*
    does heat bring out new sentences
and my old syntax changes?

BUMPER CARS

Kamakazi pilots, man your planes!
        WATCH OUT FOR THAT . . . I
speed up for small animals.
    Don't drink while driving;
        Support mental health
        or I'll kill you.
    You could spill your beer. 101
uses for a run-down wife.
        LOOK OUT! Why?
Are you coming back?
        He's bigger; take him
just about amidships . . . **with your hand**
    in someone's pants . . . and backed across
        his body 16 times . . . *must be*
reported to Help stamp out mental health;
    I'll kill you anyway.
        WHAT'S THAT ON THE ROAD?
. . . straddled across the driver's lap . . .
    A HEAD? **Quick! Slide him**
under the door to me! . . . a pregnant
    prostitute driving
an Edsel, wrong way . . . *Agnes! Agnes!*
    We can live forever!

DR. P.H.D. DARK, HYPNOTIST

Engrossing as a black hole
or your TV screen, I send out
no powers; I accept all
energies, all joys and juices. . . .

        1, 2, 3, 4, 5,
        Are your loves alive?

My cone of eclipse, this wizard's
peaked black dunce cap slips
down on your brow, the brain's
drained batteries consent. . . .

        6, 7, 8, 9, 10,
        Hope for what and when?

Cold comes to no more than
heat loss, wanting warmth;
Dark argues mere light
lacking, locked affections;

        9, 8, 7, 6, 5,
        Do numbed nerves survive?

Evil but Good's bare shortfall,
default or forfeit, be. I am
your mentor, priest, your
lover. Try opening your eyes.

        4, 3, 2, 1, 0,
        Will you waken? No.

The Carnival Girl
Darkly Attracts W. D.

O she does teach the torches to burn bright
    As a rich jewel in an Ethiop's ear.
        Romeo,
        Romeo,
      Ro' me o-ver
      In the clo-ver
    Besides, what would I say to her?
Belle qui tient ma vie
In this capture of your eyes.
    And would her mother let her out?
        And then? And then? And then?
Even as a common Italian young woman
Loaned her fresh visage to the holy mysteries,
So here, St. Anne, who's next to the Madonna,
    Donna? — that has to maybe be her name.
A glove, that I might touch that cheek
      Ham and eggs
      Between your legs;
      Mine's got meat with gravy.
Je suis aymé by her whose beauty
Surpasseth all the wonders of the earth.
      She says she ain't nice
    And what she's doing here is working.
      hath Dian's wit
And in strong proof of chastity well armed . . .
      Two and two's four; five and four's nine.
    I can piss in yours; you can't piss in mine.
Beauty too rich for use, for earth too dear.
      They were only playing leapfrog
    So Nelly, keep your belly close to mine.

A Strolling Minstrel's
Ballad of the Skulls and Flowers

Dahlia, Amaryllis, Iris,
    Flaunt their fragrance and their flair
As roman candles arc, desirous
    To burst new treasures on the air,
Spill out their color and their scent
    And whistle down the rambling bee.
When dazzle and pizzazz are spent
    And every garden's luxury
Of blossom's gone to shreds or hock,
    Where is that glamourie and that musk;
When January whips the stalk
    What memory stills the rattled husk?

By lurch and stumble, change and growth
    Struggling from all fours, we rise
Cranking the backbone up, though loath,
    To lift our skull into the skies
Where the lit eye blinks out its longing,
    Gathers the world, then from that height
Sends hosts of bright ideas thronging
    Like fireflies sparking up the night.
What are that perfume and that pollen
    Or all the brain's fine fireworks worth
Once socket, stalk and spine have fallen
    As acrid, black ash drifts to earth?

THE NOXIOUS 25¢ SONG

Drop one quarter here:
You can sweetly hear
Comfy tunes and chords
Freed from all discords,
Old familiar melodies
Curing the heart's maladies,
Comforting the soul
With music's charms. Our sole
Aim's to play you no
Ditties you don't know
Already, nothing new —
Tunes you always knew,
Words you always heard.
Join the human herd
With a two-bit piece;
Purchase pure, sweet peace.
Come home to rest; rest
Just like all the rest.

Dumbbell Rhymes

Flip it;
Flick it;
As it falls, pick it
Off, quick;
Neat trick!
Slick and steady, that's the ticket.

Spin the pin;
Haul it in;
Pause now, pirouette and pivot.
Whirl and work it
'Round the circuit
Twinkling like a red-hot rivet

Or some overwrought
Electron
Flying where you'd not
Expect one.

Dip. Don't
Slip. Don't
Trip or lose your grip.
Hurl it sheer
Twirling clear
Past the planet's atmosphere
As a comet's kept in orbit
Till the earth's mass can absorb it

Or some hot
Riled-up thought
Lustier than your mother taught you
Draws an arc
Above your cortex
Till it's drawn, dark,
Down the vortex.

Hey! I tossed it.
Wei! I lost it.
Palm it; pop it in a pocket.
Let's just stop it;
Let's just drop it;
That's enough now, I'm exhausted.

THE DRUNKEN MINSTREL
RAGS HIS BLUEGRASS LUTE

I dreamed I heard all them people say,
"Get that thing out of here; take it away.

A man who plays when days are green
May sing absurd but not obscene

Blue movie music or some tune
You'd wail under a cold blue moon.

Twang us no twangs of ill-repute;
Mama don't 'llow no bluegrass lute."

      Bluegrass was all my joy to sang;
      Bluegrass was my delight — Gol Dang!

      I'm too coarse to make common cause
      With blue stockings and their cool blue laws.

      My lute's sky-blue as a sky could be
      And shaded out toward infinity

      But I need dirt beneath my sky
      To plink it low and plunk it high.

They say, "Man winneth no awards
For words untimely, tunes untowards;

No fellowships and far fewer honors
For filthy facts and mixed up genres.

We like things simple, sweet and pure;
You play atonal, sing obscure,

Warble murder, deceit and sin;
Don't you care how square we been?"

I built this lute of blue mahiou;
That's why my quartertones turn blue.

I strung its strings from pole to pole
Over the belly and carved sound-hole,

Then blew a bubble through my nose,
A filmy globe of them and those,

A world that, twirled upon its axis,
Glitters with gritty facts and praxis.

They say, "Your song's unmentionable matter
Hurts our ears, makes our teeth chatter.

Go get your lute a coat of paint;
Jazz these things up the way they ain't.

Abstract us a whole kaleidoscope:
Red for passion, green for hope,

Purple ideas, a big pink song —
We got some rights and we ain't wrong!"

But ha-ha, this-a-way it goes:
The lily and the red, red rose,

Oh, and the black bug on the ground.
As moonshine lusters all around,

I light on lovers, traitors, rich,
Starved, what drops in the rank ditch,

The blue hues of a world of men.
It's ha-ha that-a-way, then-oh-then!

They say, "Your songs do not compute.
Your music's mixed; your moral's moot;

Your chords are foreign. We should boot
You straight out of the institute

And hire some right-minded deafmute.
Go snuff that song back up your snout;

Just get that lowdown lute right out
And don't come back, you bluegrass lout."

        Whether I yodel, jive or jazz
        Blue gives my world the hue it has

        So for my high-toned song, I smugly
        Smuggle in all things vile and ugly

        To serenade my village Venus.
        Nothing else blue can come between us.

        You all go toot your snooty flute;
        My country chords stand resolute.

        Discord and dat makes a bluegrass lute.
        I jams true blue and dat's da trut'.

Tunnel of Romance

Were you on Galapagos
When great Darwin traced the breed
To a past that's dubious?
Up, you pure and noble steed!

> Though
> So
> Slow we go,
> Tortoise-riding, tortoise-riding,
> Strong heroic types exhort us,
> > Riding on a tortoise.

Have you stormed the heavens, checked
The bounds of Heisenberg and Einstein?
Onward, till these ears detect
Some constant heartthrob or benign sign!

> Foot
> Put
> Firm as root,
> Legs like trunks of oaktrees, arching,
> Pass where fleeting visions court us,
> > Marching on a tortoise.

Were you there when Galileo
Fixed his dark specs on the sun?
Blindered now by our own *brio*
We've far-flung galaxies to outrun.

> Hep!
> Step
> With dogged pep
> Through the Inconstant Woods advancing
> With this angel to escort us,
> > Prancing on a tortoise.

Though the taper in my hand'll
Shower out sparks, not steady light,
As a squib or roman candle
Constellates the primal night,

> Hark!
> Mark:
> Though dark lies stark
> Where the Proposition's hiding,
> We'll win to Devotion's Fortress,
>> Sidling on a tortoise.

What need I to recognize
Friend from foe? I'll braille my way
With this mask before my eyes
That guarantees we'll go astray.

> Race!
> Brace
> Your carapace
> That veers like Venus' scallop surfing
> Headlong into Passion's vortice,
>> Curvetting on a tortoise.

Forth, my charger, boldly lurching
Through split affinities that bind me,
Cutting down field theories, searching
For a face that glows behind me.

> On!
> Dawn
> Must find us gone
> Like anti-matter; time grows short as
> Our own mission might abort us;
> *Non conturbat timor mortis*
>> Riding on a tortoise!

The Capture of Mr. Moon

Rocked back on his backside, not yet risen,
    It's Mr. Moon — like a thin nail paring
        Or sweet slice of some pale, blue melon —
Hauled in this tumbril, his four-wheeled prison.
    We jostle the curbsides like people staring
        At a president or some noted felon.

Like moonvines outreaching your porch's trellis
    Or a man in a child's brass bed, he lies
        With his tip and toes poked through the bars;
Not, though, to snatch at us, not to repel us.
    His thoughts have turned turtle. His eyes,
        Glozed to mirror the farthest stars,

Reflect on himself: a blue shut-in
    Cool to all sunlight as a shut-eyed
        Buddha uttering his drowsy ban.
This cage that couldn't even begin
    To hold him in, shuts us outside,
        Barring us from the Moon in the Man.

III

Each in His Season

Spring Suite

i.

The click
if lips slip
open, a little
ripple whispering
in your ear its warm
hints, first insinuations
till the clenched countryside
sighs and then relaxes far and wide
turning all trill, all rill and trickle
to the uttermost horizon; the winter's will
to rule, to cold control goes melting, melting,
the determined grip gone, juices rise and flow so
even the lightest breath, the faintest tempering air is
musky, all resolve dispersed, all limit liquidated in surrender.

ii.

This new growth's so faint it could be a
Will-o-the-wisp or vague idea —
First, the red sheathe like a suggestion
That answers, or evades, some question;
Then, out of the black soil, green shoots
Up — as if fleeing its own roots
Or something else it must have found
Terrifying in the ground:
That generations of decay,
Corruption, death, surcharge our clay;
The hankering maggot and earthworm
We all come home to, come to term;
What cravings underlie the awesome
Thrust of seed, stem, leaf and blossom.

56

iii.

One warm day: the young peartree —
a patient on a trial weekend —
ventures a stem or two, tentative
leafbuds, new color schemes; she may
forego the old restraints, that cold
solicitude of locked wards, sheets
pulled up to the chin.

A new go, all around: the meadow's
out of bankruptcy and filled with
enterprise — small field mice, moths.
Seems like we've taken on a fresh
green line of credit, vast advances
on the promise of new practices,
a sound, new management.

It's all thoroughly convincing as
a second mortgage, a second
marriage. Sap's flowing like
new currency, new lubricants.
It's plain good sense to say this
might work; history sucks; we'll
get to summer yet.

iv. A Leaf's Song

Reach; out-
stretch and over-
stress till the tuned string
sing with tension;
till the wrung taut drumhead
hum, rimshot
crack and ring;
so the guy-wired tent's skin

tense and wrack tight, distending
cable and strung tendon,
a suspension
bridge that ends
no where
but slack and empty air —
springboard, trampoline and net
to catch and bounce back
the pranking young sun
there.

V.

As a steamed-over mirror
Unfades and gets clearer,
Spring's deepening polaroid
Face informs the void
Grey scumbled scene.
Warm rains bring their green
Transfusions; faint hues,
Hints of pink, the blues
Of newborns' wraps infuse
Sky and ditch while the willow
Breathes a hazy yellow
Aureole or halo.
Yet somehow in a twinkling
This still pool, our unwrinkling
Looking glass, reflects
What's here with what comes next:
An ocean churning, tossed
Till every feature's lost
And all forms are deep-sixed.
A film that can't be fixed.

vi.

Through rocky shale, our sapling
dogwood with sure power
drives down thin roots, grappling
for sustenance and mooring,
to swell leaf, bud and flower
like a warm air balloon
that lifts with the soft stirring
of errant wind and weather,
falls back then in a swoon
and yet recovers soon
to rise, past all securing,
then strain at its frail tether.

vii.

Battling for the sun, young ash
and maples take up the choice
locations, shading their neighbors out.
Both crow and owl devour
each other's young, while later species
move in — swarms of convict colonists
and outcasts spread across the land.
Nestlings shrilling to be fed, the roughnecks
flourish, the smaller or more timid
are never much missed. Things
settle down; we'll be someone
respectable as the year moves on.

viii.

D'ja read me?
C'mere!
D'ja hear me?
Ya need me!

Through April's fields, small butterflies
Primp like barrettes or bright bow ties
That disappear as punk-spiked starling
Flocks come hang out, squealing, quarreling:

Don't leap for less;
Jump my springs.
These wings, this crest
Got everything.

In clashing yellows, oranges, greens
The land goes lewd and loud as teens
That turn up tapes, plug in this year's
Top tunes to batter at their ears:

I lose least;
Sing songs strongest.
I got the lust
Lasts you longest.

Snarled in the grasses, wild strawberries
Shine bright as scabs where thick, dark hair is,
Like fireflies or the afterspark
Of roaches lit where strange cars park:

I get more faster;
Gain most ground.
My nest's hung best.
Don't fuck around.

In all our nubile dells and dingles
The young pulse swings, the nerve end tingles;
The same old brand new lies and jingles
Wring out the brains of Spring's worst singles:

D'ja hear me?
C'mere!
D'ja read me?
Ya need me!

ix.

Now robins' eggs betray the hue
Of Andrew Marvell's drop of dew
Reflecting heaven and Mary's cloak of blue

Clear as some super-Aryan eye
Bright with its vision of a sky
Where nestlings scramble up to fly
Dogfights for wealth and mastery by and by.

Soon these blue bloods will spurn the plain
Earth, foul the seas and burn the grain;
Like tattoos or the mark of Cain,
Heaven's image newborn in the brain
Brands us for charnel fires again.

SUMMER SEQUENCE

i.

Every young plant springing
        into heavy air,
                this flinging
one's self up, out
        from the core
                as if earth's got
too hot
        for anyone to touch
                too much;
much as the much-sung lark
        climbs higher,
                outsinging where
branches spread and flare
        like ravelled wire-
                ends or one's hair
in an electric charge might
        upstand, lift, as some
                wire prancer's parasol
might parachute and drift
        you gentle down to ground
                once more.

ii.

All night black tree
shapes wrestled their dark
angels or assailants; the deep woods
wracked by shattering, cracking;
then rain drove straight
sheets like a wave's crash
wrenching leaves and birds' nests

from the branch, battering
grain flat in the fields;
mice, rabbits in their burrows
drowned.
      At first dawn, soft
mists down the valley rise till
light strikes, enamelling
each emerald green leaf
splattered clean.

iii.

Up this hillside, through patches
of scrub and brush, green catches
on as fire or virus spreads
through unsuspecting heads —
a new belief, the fashion
and excuse for passion.

These towering beeches crowd
on foliage like a proud
ship's canvas that must fear,
still envious, still near,
those vessels it's outrun
for its place in the sun.

Our orchard, woods and meadow
now breathe out the credo
and pieties of growth;
those who've survived seem loathe
to find luxuriance less
than just reward and progress.

Even the ongoing brook
can't spare nerve now to look
back at what's been drowned,

what's gaining on it, bound
to jail it up at last —
the dry bones of its past.

IV.

As cock orioles lock
        beaks and, orange
                slash-and-dart wings
battering, flail the sky;
        as flyweight fighter-
                pilot, laser-
throated humming-
        birds climb each
                above each other
then dive down, drive
        each other off; fierce,
                piercing as the arc
of an acetylene torch,
        or the hand-struck
                spark that might
ignite and scorch the eye,
        here the buck bunting,
                indigo, his million
prisms scattering
        shattered white light
                blue, blue, blue
homes in through
        the startled air,
                a tracer or some
riled-up, forge-
        bright rivet
                to its mark.

V.

Green; we're eager for you, green;
The garden gone green; green for Go;
Cresses floating where brook water's clean;
The fireflies' code to spark night's scene;
The dead log's phosphorescent glow.

Now the beret and uniform
of creeping vines and tendrils swarm
over each boulder and rock wall,
past barren slate and up the tall
oak trunks. Soon, all they'll let you see
bends to green's rule and currency,
finding somewhere some shred or rag
of green to hang out for a flag
declaring our sincere, complete
complicity in our defeat.

Green; we're greedy for you, green;
The corn field grown green; green for Go;
Thick duckweed in the watertank;
The bankroll buying out the bank
While mildew, mold and mosses grow.

vi.

In broad daylight, the fat
deer — two fawns and a doe —
amble our old orchard, nibbling
the appletrees' twigs and shoots,
the leafbuds off our blueberries,
all stems and tender growth.
Flagrant, frumpish; not even
our dog's stench drives them out —
walking awkwardly, the haunches

hinged like mismatched tie rods.
     Perish all thought of bound,
soar, breakfree — the élan of flight.

vii.

Another leaf
     and who needs it?
Another attempt,
     a stem, a leafbud
breaks from the branch
     in sunlight, then
that light's gone.

One flower
     more or less
to what point?
     More sap drops squeezed
to plump and fill
     ten million seedpods
others will devour.

More suckers slink out
     from the redbud's root;
more bulbs impact
     the crowded ground;
one more root crammed
     down through tired clay
and broken stone.

viii. Cabbage Butterflies

Paired like square vanes
  spinning in some sun-
    spun, glass-globed top,
they orbit their closed
  system, lifting off
    the meadow grasses
high and higher and
  then flutter down
    apart, yet rejoined,
climb twirling like
  a bolo's ends, as twin
    stars or ice skaters
csardas, caught in
  one another's gravity
    till all earth's
greater weight winds
  every urge and engine
    down. Why don't
  we go
upstairs?

ix.

  Deregulated summer rolls on:
Our meadow's making hay as if
  the national gross product must be
grass, the duty of all flesh: get high
  as your eye by the Fourth of July.

  Fledged, open-eyed, the rough young
bluejays squall like soccer fans
  crammed in their twiggy stadium — loud
disciples of some rock star, cure-all
  politics or new saviour: greed.

Nothing will come of nothing; things
lead to things: the ad campaign's still
        on though the summer's till brims over.
Sunflowers smile down like visitors
        to Plato's Cave or brazen bank examiners,

        where shameless, coarse young leaves spread
open to the sun. Through ditch and hedgerow
        kudzu carries out its hostile
takeover; the greenback reigns. Our
        scriptures: lovecharts, popcharts and the Dow.

X.

The loitering red-tail screeches,
        Redoubled in the pond,
Then tools off down the valley and
        Beyond, beyond, beyond. . . .

Locust and katydid grind on
        Like the whirr where distant foundries
Work all three shifts. Thick brambles spread
        Over all known boundaries.

Fireflies, rising in the fields, blip
        The darkening screen to chart
Another ring laid on the trees,
        More fat around the heart.

Autumn Variations

i.

The evening grosbeak on the lawn
Will turn his back on us, move on
With his wide family and those friends
We thought were ours. That's how it ends.
If it's been good, be glad it's been;
It won't be. The cold shoulder's in.
We must make do, once summer's done,
With our fair weather friends or none.

ii.

The garden's garter snake,
the warty toad in our garage
don't get around these days.
Woodchuck and rabbit sink
into themselves; if they
have some idea, who's to say?
The few birds left accept
the mob opinions
and the fashions: a dull
Stalinist grey that will
offend no one. The turtles
turntail on the pond, withdraw
to meditate, regroup or,
joining what's too big to beat,
dig down in the numb
security of clay, one
with their fate.

iii.

In spray-paint, psychedelic, gaudy,
Fall scrawls its name — a blunt and bawdy
Challenge to the complacent wood.
We say: there goes the neighborhood;
It is not and it cannot come to good.
Soon, flustered leaves will sag like torn
Wallpaper; solid dark walls, worn
Through here and there, expose a bitter
Sky while, on the bare ground, litter
And stub ends pile up everywhere.
Not even one green plant would dare
Poke its nose out in that crude air
Of catch-as-catch-can thievery, lust,
Cut-throat protection and sick trust.
Where year by year we walked together
Determined paths, a wilder atmosphere
Wheels in, flaunting its chains, blades and black leather.

iv.

Imperial greenery withdraws,
flamboyant and corrupt; the leaf's
far government's lost
faith in its mission, that certainty
to be despotic and
victorious. Now failure's
certain, a certain
mercy enters in; such as
it is, the sun
gets spread around, the magnanimity
of the poor. Only some pines,
hard-needled loyalists, cling
to their colors and won't change. Dark,
under those implacable branches,
nothing grows.

v.

Maple and ash in the hedgerow
Figure the green light's gone and go
To a flat brown. The white-tailed deer
Must know what's up; they disappear
Like high ideals. Across the field,
Mallows and black-eyed susans yield
To the solicitude of tractor
And combine, like a trash compactor
Crushing the summer's shapes and scents —
Leaf, stem and petal — into dense
Blocks scattered like packed bags and crates
Around the field while the field waits.

vi.

Sharp, black crickets
have got the house
surrounded; miners and sappers
gnaw our siding;
buckwheat flies, wasps
and spiders — spies —
thread the cellar and the walls.
And these are the deserters
who've lost the front
outside. Put on fat;
put on fur; the windows
rattle. The only news
says we'll know soon
what sort of man you are.

vii.

Bark strips peel off the sycamore
Like weathered clapboards. The wind's war
Moves up closer. Our woodlot's floor
Fills up with wreckage like a village
Fought and recaptured. Ripe for pillage,
Berries and haws shine down a street
Where the raccoon and field mouse beat
A long, inglorious retreat.

viii.

Bare bones! bare bones!
is the wind's suggestion
and, one by one, leaves
like bright embroidery
rinsed in bleach or like
words in the brain's skein,
the tree of memory,
are gone. All sweet details
pass on in "the abstraction
of old age": skeletal
trunk and branchings, lacy
tracework of each leaf,
medulla and the neural reach
of those ways we once knew
things we forget
under the soft, featureless
democracy of snow.

SNOW SONGS

i.

one. now another. one
more. some again; then done.
though others run
down your windshield when
up ahead a sudden
swirl and squall comes on
like moths, mayflies in a swarm
against your lights, a storm
of small fry, seeds, unknown
species, populations — every one
particular and special; each one
melting, breaking, hurling on
into the blank black. soon
never to be seen again.
most never seen.
all, gone.

ii.

First, the exhausted, brown
leaves, then the snow comes down
the way a year's change shakes
hairs loose or those dull flakes
littering your shoulder.
Soon, windier and colder
gusts — as confetti falls
on our sunstruck festivals,
then, flurrying wilder, thicker,
scatters like heavy ticker-
tape over the parade
route and the motorcade

of some departing hero.
Now, into a near-zero
visibility
where nothing can be
known sure of events,
what with the pervasive, dense
smother of shredded documents.

iii.

White out; white out; so
        that the landscape's ledger
                balances again.
On the hill, the white-tailed deer's
        remains are spirited
                away like laundered funds.
flesh, pelt and all
        the inner workings nibbled
                down, salted away inside
the general, unmentionable,
        unseen economy of the woods.
                Bones, like the broken branches,
soften, sink back down
        in ground that sent them
                out to reconnoitre.
Soon this whole, broad
        Stalingrad will be no more
                than scattered fading photographs,
just some aging soldiers'
        recollections till at last
                all thought dies down to the
perfection of the blank page
        and the lighted
                screen that will flick off.

iv.

The leading colonists of summer,
Carriers of what we called progress,
        Uplift, or flat success,
Have gone south taking their plunder.
        All crucial witnesses

Are safely hushed-up underground
Or live on on the season's scraps.
        Thick snow blots out the maps;
The woods, the air, the memory's found
        Compromised by gaps.

We're left with dwindled and diminished
Hopes, left with those hangers-on
        Too listless to get gone,
With long abandoned, half-finished
        Plans, conclusions drawn.

v.

The horizon, a maternal flour sifter,
Sprinkled your landscape; light winds lifted
Powdered sugar in your bowl; the drifting
Snow, white tissue paper for your gifts.

Now, coke on glass, powder on pocked cheeks; foam
On lip, lake, contact points; abundant mold
On the peaches, bird dung on the civic stones;
Whitewash, whitewash over Holy Wisdom's dome.

vi.

Now snow lies level
    with the windowsills. Along
the thruway, traffic
    like fresh water flows
between banks ten feet
    above our heads. Still
it sifts down slow
    as infinite, small
skeletons of diatoms drift,
    settling through the salt seas,
falling only inches year
    by year, some 20,000 species,
geometric, crystalline, no
    two shells alike, covering
the sea's floor hundreds
    of feet deep. Now turn
the radio up louder; try to
    catch the local dialect.

vii.

8,000,000 *alleluias* or
lace paper valentines, these
bitsy webs and doilies —
such dear wee scallops
on each twig, a sweet
tiara for each flower. Oh,
vast crochet hooks of the
skies, God's bobbin mills,

tat us this day our peekaboo
bra and scanties; glamorize
the gamey soiled loins of
one more incontinent season;
fall, plastic popcorn, pack
and seal the year up, draw
this dull white coverlet
over the patient's eyes.

viii.

Leaving the snow
        bank, your boot leaves
                a fossil print — an
emptiness remains. Just so,
        across the field you've made
                a trail of vacancies.
        Still the snow
falls — as a clean sheet smooths
                your shape out of the bed
        you don't go back to.
                You are the missing
        tooth, the one place
at the table, lost
                wax from the casting — though,
        while they last,
these chicken scratchings hold
                the voice unspoken on
        the finished page as under
                plaster hardening,
a fading face.

IV

Dance Suite, Et Alia

More for McGraw

Minuet in F##

— Melody: Beethoven's Minuet in G

In the dance, should glances chance to get
      Lewd and wet,
      Minuet;

For entranced romance whose stance won't let
      People pet,
      Minuet;

Though the girl you whirl and twirl may fret,
      Overhe't,
      Minuet;

Find a norm that's formal, warm and yet
      Little threat;
      Minuet.

    With some stranger you've met,
        Like a man with debts, then,
        Hedge your bets, men:

Guide that deep-sighed, sloe-eyed, sly coquette;
      Don't just sweat:
      Minuet.

W. D. AND THE DARK COMEDIAN
SEARCH FOR HAPPY FAMILIES

It's like the soul:
                everyone
is joyously convinced
he's got one; others
may have doubts. Here,
on the operating table,
all doubts dissolve.
You go on quartering
the peach to find
its flavor, dismantling
computers to reach
a text. These houses
have windows as open
as benign smiles
to the street. We pass
through, top to bottom,
and pass on. Today:
incestuous sheets,
the lovers at each other's
jugular, the beard sandwich
in the icebox and a child
chained in the basement,
raging. Insanity:
                it's like
genitals. You never
see or mention them; they're
there.

Mr. Evil Disguises Himself as Herself — with Murder in Her Heart for W. D.

— Melody: The Stripper

Note the elegance of line,
The grass skirt gestures and the fine
      seduc-
      tive bi-
      as of
      the torso,
Slim as a palm tree;
      even more so,

Check this precious, heart-shaped bib
At the breast cage and the rib
      suggest-
      ing heart-
      felt pas-
      sion; watch
These arrows pointing
      to the crotch.

Time to welcome our Miss Treavle,
Shaped with all some daughter of Eve'll
      give
      a man,
      then when
      she's had 'im,
Drive him forth, stripped
      stark as Adam

Through the flaming gates of Eden.
What need I repair to Sweden?
             I'll drag
             up my
             new clothes
             exchange
Into something rare and sex-strange.

Here, I rise up from the norm
Decked out in my own trans-form —
             design-
             er flanks
             in slate-
             grey denims,
Sleek as a cobra
             steeped in venoms,

Then slink up the swaying ladder
To his roost, lithe as an adder,
             while black
             thoughts swarm
             around
             my head,
Crooning like gnats, "I'll
             knock him dead!"

Mr. Evil Humiliates W. D.
with Child-like Toys

Here's to thee, as a maker skilled
    In fine construction, as a spouse
In husbandry, as one to build
    Strong joints and long ties — here's a house
Scaled to a family of dolls,
    Complete in all details and lacking
Only the fourth of its four walls,
    All firm foundations or sound backing.
        Accept this honor, you who've got
        Both arms tied in a granny knot.

Recognizing you truly are
    A pioneer whose boundary-scorning
Drive to explore will take you far,
    To save walking it every morning,
May I present this coaster wagon
    With three of its four wheels to carry you
Swift as a chariot to your agon,
    Then haul you back slow and bury you.
        Please mount this tumbril, you who ride
        Backwards wherever I decide.

Saluting your deep dedication
    To steady pursuit of one goal,
Enduring love — in celebration
    Of your capacious, virile soul,
Here's Ken and Barbie, perfect dolls
    Who've learned love's real nice and can last
Though lacking heart or genitals
    Like Satan on ice, fixed and fast.
        Receive this tribute, you whose face
        Is blue with cold and blank disgrace.

Fox Trot: The Whisper, the Whistle and the Song

— Melody: Whispering

Whispering to hypnotize a hearer,
Whistling to lip and lure you nearer,
Listening to know if your thoughts mirror
    Each word and note
    As a bird learns by rote
    To follow.

Lilting my lyric blue and moodily,
Lisping to purse the lips out shrewdly,
Lingering on wet and warm sounds lewdly,
    Till you'll fulfill
    Every whim of my will
    To win you;

Whimpering to cage your thoughts in pity,
Tempering your hearing to my ditty,
Simpering to veil the nitty-gritty:
    That you'll abandon
    Your vision and all
    You planned on;

Whispering to tune out all resistance,
Whistling to fix your course and distance,
Witnessing how my song's persistence
    Whisks you to my
        Isle
        Of
        View.

For John and Carol Wood.

Mr. Evil Waltzes W. D.'s Thought
Away from Cock Robin

— Melody: Tales from the Vienna Woods

A question,
            an answer,
suggestion
            or glance, sir,
a yellow skirt that ghosts down the
hallways of the heart;

a shape that
            wafts, flirting
thin drapes like
            a curtain
that opens on dark gardens and
breezes lift apart;

to twirl and
            entrance, sir,
that girl-formed
            young dancer,
her arms around my ears where sweet
birdsong once would start;

one chance to
            romance her,
one hand's in
            her pants, sir,
progressing through fixed patterns to the
pulse of love's low Art.

Mexican Hat Dance

— Melody: Jarabe Tapatio

When you're wearing a big, broad sombrero,
If your brain and your aims remain narrow,
You can mate right and left like a sparrow
  Or go trampling your friends in the dirt.

In a sweetly old-fashioned sunbonnet,
You can turn the world pat as a sonnet
And enforce your opinions upon it
  Though you neither instruct nor divert.

In a Puritan's flat hat or "waffle,"
You can find the round world's just gawdawful
And then flatly proclaim it unlawful
  To feed well, fool, fiddle or flirt.

    When a fat,
    Well-fed cat
    Dons a hat
  And believes it's a halo there,
    He can splat
    You as flat
    As a sprat
  Since by fiat he's just and fair.

In a tall, mitred hat like a bishop,
There are plenty of dogmas to dish up,
Not to mention the rules you can fish up
  And the powers you can swiftly assert.

If you're wearing Raskolnikov's high hat,
Lifting all your low drives to the sky, at
The moment you get folks to buy that,
  The axe falls and somebody gets hurt.

When a brat
Pulls a gat
In a spat
And proclaims virtue's on his side,
He can rat
In combat,
Quick as that,
Since *his* bloodlust's been justified.

If you're wearing warpaint and a feather
Or a jacket of steel-studded leather,
Just the same, better cover your nether
        Extremes with a lead-shielded skirt

For the world keeps earphones in its helmet
To be sure that you don't overwhelm it
And your sharpest attacks will be well met
        With a potency far from inert.

So take off all these helmets, quixotic,
Or you'll turn a pyrotic neurotic,
Patriotic, narcotic, hypnotic, despotic,
        Idiotical con- or per- vert.

MEDLEY: MORTAL LOVE WATCHES THE DANCE

— Melody: Various 1930's Love Songs

That cold, blue magic's caught them in its spell,
That siren sound out of a sax's bell:

> You press the first valve down;
> The blood begins to bulge and pound;
> In the music's windy surge they've found
> The pulse that makes the brain go 'round.

They'd be satisfied
To orbit, side by side,
Athwart the sluice of time and tide

> Forever
> And never;
> Sunday, Monday and always.

For all they know they may never meet again
In thunder, lightning, spite or rain.

> You press the last valve down
> And the circuits close; their springs are wound
> To the music's key and the pitch they want. They
> Seem so light on the storm's breath, bound
> Together over the swirling ground
> Till the tune ends
> *La bocca mi bacio' tutto tremante*
> And it soon ends
> Below, below, below.

> Although

They dream in vain, in the bowels it will remain
Like a leaf that's caught in the tide

Or the drain

While many a lying lover's lain
In back rooms and dark hallways.

MASQUERADA: NEITHER THE HEAT OF THE MASK NOR THE POINT OF THE HOUSE CAN DISTRACT W. D. FROM MR. EVIL DISGUISED

— Melody: 16th century Masquerada for Lute

He: High on my tower I perch
Like the peaked steeple of a church
Scouting the dark
Like an airfield's sock
Or my own weathercock.

She: I orbit 'round the roost
Where you rotate, serenely goosed;
As an electron
Skates through its arc,
I circle like a shark.

Both: Like dancing,
Entranced things —
Or dogs in the park.

He: My cheeks and forehead flush
With a pink, pyromantic blush
Seared by this mask
I project in place:
A red-hot poker face.

She: My face is true cool blue
Flamed with rouge as I offer you
Your own tower's cute
Doll-sized counterpart
Or phallic tootsie-tart.

Both: Fixed tenser
Than fencers,
We're closer apart,

Unseen, though deeply felt,
Each one's reaching below the belt,
Hoping to grope
While we hold aloof
This groined, cold-weatherproof

    Green delta-
    Formed shelter
Or portable roof.

Hip Hop

Lined up
Girls and boys,
Coins in the drop slot; wind up toys;
Necks that switch
Every which way;
Join the Hip Hop, rapping like a robot.

Streets full of busfumes; stairs full of shovin';
TV's full of promises: luxuries and lovin';
Oil's on the water; spray's on the pumpkin;
Aspirin's full of strychnine, cyanide or somethin'.

Wig-wag
Knee joints,
Elbows crimped to zig-zag points;
Wrists and ankles
Twisted into angles;
Splayed-out fingers clamping into fists.

Sidewalks full of garbage; pictures in the news;
Mayor's on the radio spouting out excuses;
Bars on the storefronts; landlord's on the way;
Cops've got their Spring list — they'll make it pay.

Nuts and bolts
Charged by volts
Jumpstart into spastic jerks and jolts;
Gears and notches
Grinding crotches,
Juicing up the parts of the fools that watch us.

Ground's full of chemicals; ocean's full of waste;
Brother's full of steroids; meat's got no taste;
Ceilings full of roaches; rats around the cradle;
Everybody's learned to read the lies on the label.

Swirl around,
Clown, on the ground,
Twirling like a dervish whirls, upside down;
Legs there,
Kicking in the air,
Striking like scorpions or Medusa hair.

A bullet's in the chamber; needle's in the vein;
Leg's set in plaster; no time for pain;
Street's full of dealers; girls are on the curbs;
Make a killing fast and head out for the suburbs.

Shift your shoulder
Like a soldier
Ant, an identical mannikin or clone;
Who can hurt a tall doll
Rigid and mechanical
Dancing to the dictates of a microphone?

Tango: W. D. Is Dwarfed by the Vision of Mr. Evil with Cock Robin

— Melody: La Cumparsita

Turn
That
Red-
Breast
Loose

     before I faint, sir;

          Cease
          This
          Vile
          A-
          Buse

     and foul constraint, sir;

Ne-
Ver
Dare
Se-
Duce,

     pervert and taint, sir,

          Tar-
          Nish
          Or
          Tra-
          Duce

     those souls you mayn't, sir.
        When
        You
        Touch
        Things
     in this lewd tango,
        Paw
        And
        Clutch
        Things,

pure spirits can grow
    Soiled
    By
    Such
    Things.
No matter
    How
    You
    Paint
      yourself to
be a saint,
    You
    Ain't.

I'm incensed; this situation
Could drive a person to frustration;
    I'll set my foot right down,
    Ordering, Stop!
      Then scowl
    Or call a cop.
Being faced by such a monster,
How can I make a fit response? —
    My grief
    Can't be endured?
    Fie, thief,
    Unhand that bird?
My whole position
    Grows absurd.

How can I face this abduction?
Is this rape or just seduction?
Whatever else, it's destruction
Of the things a man holds dear.
    I feel so small,
    So limp and weak,
    I don't dare call
    Or scarcely speak;
    I'll smirk and crawl

Like some pipsqueak
Or meek, wimp sneak
Who'd turn the
other cheek —
Poor
Freak!

Dav-
Id
Once
Lacked
Size
but kept reliant
On
Things
Strong
And
Wise
not pale and pliant;
Right
Be-
Tween
The
Eyes
he drilled that giant.
Let's
Rare
Up,
A-
Rise
fierce and defiant:
"Set
That
Bird
Down
and that's an order.
Clear
Out

                  Of
                  Town;
head for the border.
                  Don't
                  Snarl
                  Or
                  Frown;
                            Noli me
                  Tan-
                  Ge-
                  Re.
                        Just make your
getaway.

                  Don't
                  Stay."

APACHE: MISS TREAVLE PURSUES W. D.

— Melody: the common "apache" dance

Don't;
       Don't;
              Don't;
Don't give up on little Me;
        MA 'AM
                 Ay,
       Ay,
     I
Been as rotten as can be;
        AM
        That I'd desert you,
        Hurt you,
        Then do you dirt, too —

No,
       No;
             No
Way a good girl ought to act;
        HAM
              True
        Blue
      You
Been to me and that's a fact.
        LAMB
        Why should I want to
        Haunt you,
        Shoot you down, then taunt you?
        SHAM

Why
       Lie? —
             I
Talked about it with my shrink.

WHAM
                He . . .
          Me . . .
      We
Soon can iron out every kink,
       BAM
       Each mental set or
       Fetter;
       He thinks I'm better.

Too
       True,
            You
Ought to leave me like the rest.
       SLAM
              Go
         Slow,
       Though;
After all I just confessed
       SCRAM
       You won't be cruel;
       You will
       Find that I'm your jewel.
       DAMN

Tap Dance: W. D. Escapes from Miss Treavle

— Melodies: Fit as a Fiddle, Greensleeves
and The Leaves So Green

Loose as a linnet and fresh out of love,
I could jump jail walls and lark any dove,
    Groin slaves us all may join;

Green, black and 21, bird out of hand,
I beat no bushes; I'm beating the band.
    Grim leapers, dismayed, dull-eyed;

On my way out, now, I'm getting wooed;
Never been kissed but ostensibly screwed.
    Dream thieves always hard-up, cold

My Lady Belle-tone Bim swings to the dong;
Wing out wild Bimbo, go gang your own gong.

    Groin slaves us all may join;
    Grim leapers, dismayed, dull-eyed;
    Dream thieves always hard-up, cold
        Among the sleeves so green, oh!

The Memory of Cock Robin Dwarfs W. D.

"Each single wing-
        éd thing
is terrible," said Rilke who
    had known a few.
    Brahms, too:

"You can't know how
        even now
our ears ring with that fellow's strong
    wingbeat and song."
    We long,

    like Semele,
        to see
what held us close only last night,
    but in pure light
    our sight,

    tired and refined,
        goes blind.
Too much of sounds we yearn to hear
    can numb the ear;
    that dear-

    ly lovéd throat's
        charged notes
can overload our circuits, thrill
    and fuse the will
    they kill

    then, when they're gone,
        ring on.
Still, if that voice that overjoyed
    me were destroyed,
    the void

would make me shrink
to think
and never shape one note or word
matching that bird
once heard.

W. D. Studies the Spectra of Departure

In the perspective of the heart,
Those dearly loved, when they depart,
Take so much of us when they go
That, like no thing on earth, they grow
Larger when fleeing from the eye
Till they invest the vacant sky
With their dear presence, an existence
Lost in love's exponential distance:
They're our astronomy, our science
And starry myth; they are red giants.
As for ourselves who have been left
Behind, we find we've been bereft
Of our best being, of the whole
Mass that could matter to the soul;
This sort of thing can leave you blue.
And whether our pale, bloodless hue
Arises from the Arctic chill
Of energies that flared out — will,
Warmth and acetylene desires —
Or from excess of passion, fires
Turned in, we seem an endomorph
Of shrunken hopes; we're our white dwarf.
By loss of qualities, we are
Changed into a neutron star
Or part-time partner, off and on;
Worse still, we may recount what's gone
Until, self-justified by grief,
We're turned a sum-and-substance thief,
Drain and devour what dares come near,
Emptying all things we hold dear,
Till we collapse inside at last,
Taking all we've drawn with us, past
Recall, recovery or control,
Down our own depths as a black hole.

The Forces of Love Re-assemble W. D.: Instructions

1. Let lust, screwed over, screw on to trust
    That just must rise out of doubt and dust.

2. Let urge, now bound, rebound to surge
    Past boundary, self's verge, then to merge.

3. Let verve, pale letch, latch onto nerve
    Perversely leaning into curve or swerve.

4. Let tongue link throat, join groin and lung
    That the stunned, stung, far-flung world be sung.

5. Let soul, withdrawn, fill up the whole
    Gap, role gone, goal gone, and regain control.

6. Let blood, valve-locked, scummed over, thud
    With tides, roil, broil, scud to full flood.

7. Let heart impart impulse and art
    That Eden's eve, that Adam's applecart
    Once stopped, dropped silent and apart, start.

W. D. Sees Himself Animated

Open your eyes, now, W. D.;
This is your life. If such there be.

Here is the infant, scarcely three,
Seated, enthroned in sovereignty
    Over his ball, like a world made free;
    This is your life if such there be.

Here comes a sneaky snake whose head,
Tongue and long fangs are blood-red,
Creeping his way with oozy tread
    Up to that pleased and curious boy
    Who reaches out for this fine new toy
        That brightens the peaceful nursery;
        This is your life if such there be.

There the bird flies whose face of green
And strong wings hover above the scene
With beak and talons to contravene
And battle his ancient, serpentine
    Brother and foe whose slack lips smiled
    With cool, dry malice that quite beguiled
    The poor little innocent stupid child
Stuck stock-still as a hoptoad there
Perched on the edge of his painted chair
        And crowned with a dunce-cap, fittingly.
        This is your life if such there be.

You are yourself who stands aside
To watch and witness, petrified,
While vast universal powers collide
In archetypal conflict to decide
Whether good fortune or ill betide,
    Whether the robin with green face
    Would clench its claws in the wriggling, base

Adder, then soar, all craft and grace,
Over your checkerboard of days
Or should the serpent, sleek and wily,
Slink through to its goal where it might slyly
Envenom the growing young boy vilely,
 Who sits like a stone grown soft with moss
 Seeming to take no thought of loss
  And making no move toward victory.
  This is your life if such there be.

These are the long, white puppet strings
That lead to some hidden source that brings
Spirit to move all living things:
Whatever hisses, crawls and stings;
Whatever veers or glides, then sings;
All but you — you wait in the wings
 Wondering what primeval laws
 Govern this stage and what it was
 In malignant forces that could cause
 The heart that faces the dragon's jaws
 To freeze fast, and what warmth then thaws
The pausing mind; what passion stirred
The broad-winged, brilliant-feathered bird
To fill our skies, like creation's word,
With songs such as mortals never heard;
 What in the psyche could awake
 Powers so fell as the sneaky snake
 Then turn them loose, and what could make
The child, with one red foot and hand
And one of green, rise up and stand
 Erect, responding suddenly:
  "I speak for the bird who sang for me,"
  So that's your life. If such there be.

COCK ROBIN ESCAPES FROM THE ALIZARIN OF EVENING

Out of the eggshell, fearlessly rocketting,
Out of the iron-clad, studded steamertrunk of dusk,
Up from the autumn twilight, half-lit shy light where
    the fledgling whistled his moony tunes,
Out of the virginal vigil where the Troubadour tootled
    a tremulous kazoo,
Out of the blue *cantilena*, crepuscular and gooey,
From the sobbing, throbbing, yearning, burning, trilling,
    shrilling, self-fulfilling willingness to be kept,
Out of Love's capitalism, the four-square caged and cornered
    market
Where value lies in scarcity, virtue in poverty and the payoff
    sucks,
Past the *verismo* canary of self-induced ejaculation
By Don Juan who don't want none and Leporello totting up
    the ones that got away,
Into the vast blast furnace,
Into the mottled, clotted-blood-black cauldron roiling factory
    smoke and flame,
Into the mill foundry where, fulfilled, the unwilled act is
    founded,
I, Cock of the Waking, Robin, robbed of self-flakery, robed in *bel
    canto*'s naked and complete steel,
Into midnight's crucible and corona, zing.

To Shape a Song

It's not quite
          a kite,
not just like folding
          origami — though much is
implicate, implicit,
          closed in on itself,
                              yet it
unfurls its breadth on
          thin air like
the heron's wing or the heart's
          loyalty;
                    not paper planes
          not even one that soars
down through the auditorium,
          glides,
                    veers and rides
over the performers' startled
                              heads
          and even bearing
                    BRAVO
for its name;
                    not altogether
a windsock or spinnaker
          though it must belly
out to breezes and must be controlled
          by winds it can't; not
even a windmill's great vanes
          though its stones grind fine
and it can lift you up
                    swift
you in your makeshift armor
          then deposit you

yards off,
     aching,
         out
of breath;
    not even then.

V

In Flower

In Flower

i. Snow Drops

Spring's first whispers
Though in winter's tongue:
Frosty globes hung above green
Leaves and thawed ground like
Lamps left on all day
To tell us dark and cold
Are never far
And neither green nor gold
Nor icy white can stay
Here long. Or stay away.

ii. Colt's Foot 𝄞

Along the roadside ditches
1000 little mirrors
where the sun
can recognize flamboyance
and flounce across their blue
stage like a rock star,
raucous, lewd and sovereign
above their beaming
screaming
faces.

iii. Tulips

Tight green buds
   like fists or as
a newborn's skull around
   its fontanelle
might fill and swell out —
   opened halves of
some bright eggshell
   or the gaping bills
where young birds squall
   and trill above their
mud-dull nest and still
   unfolding petals
stretch up, out and over
   backwards: a stemmed
and blown glass goblet's
   spread lips that outspill
their brimming overflow
   to wish you well.

iv. Dandelions ⸙

Some Viking's blond shock;
   one sun-flare of a whetted edge
across our suburban's clipped lawn;
   one settler, two, and then
the grey-haired, smoke-soft afterburst
   remains: a spook transmitter
disperses intermittent sniping
   till the whole broad yard erupts
in small arms fire, the firing
   off of neurons through the brain's
dark networks, and the field
     is taken.

v. Bearded Iris ⚘

All labial folds and ripples
    like the wavy edge of some
        Victorian candy dish,
the ridges of brain coral or
    flamenco dancer's hemline
        flared out, arching overhead,
the lapping shawl and mantle
    of a manta ray, these petals,
bearded, curling as a wet,
        warm tongue spreads smoothing,
    soothing all refusal
down.

vi. Touch-Me-*NOT*

Jewelweed, gem-set
or enamelled basket
earrings, light wired,
dazzling at some dancer's
cheek and soft throat,
inviting, offering
NOTHING
to the hand;
still tossing in the
warmed breeze beckoning to
Stand Back
Close!

vii. Narcissus

A gold tall teacup
        on its splayed-out saucer
            offering
no handle, nothing
        to the lip but
            sheer form;
or yellow Deco
        telephone that answers
            nothing back,
yet if you'd learned
        its cipher, could thread
            your question down
dark circuits
        to the center
            echoing.

viii. Geraniums

The muscular coarse tendrils out-
    reaching every which way —
branchings that must be pinched
    back or the overswarming
plant grows lank and gangly,
    its energies exhausted in
expansion, spindled out, infertile.
    The pruned leaves, thick and
common as a laborer's tough palm.
    The flowers uplifted on those
hedged limbs like a mob's fists
    upraised and shaking, a snake's
tail rattling, like clatterbones,
    like dice.

ix. Peonies ₹

The leaves, ellipses: prints
    of cool green lips — most of them
doubled, some flawed. The whole
    bush crouched down null, inert,
somehow expectant, somehow gathering
    critical mass and thrust.

Trajectory: a tracer scoring
    the night sky, uplifting
buds still sheathed. But over
    and across them, black ants
pass like shiverings, touching,
    opening — the rocket bursts

full flower heads on the abyss,
    a rush of fresh blood flushing
the cheeks' glow, the excited
    mouth. Yet one breath more,
and petals, withering, fading,
    fall, all features gone.

₹

ACKNOWLEDGMENTS

Grateful acknowledgment is made to the editors and publishers of publications in which poems (or earlier versions of them) first appeared:

Agenda: "The Sealchie's Son";

The American Poetry Review: "House of Horrors," "A Strolling Minstrel's Ballad of the Skulls and Flowers" and "The Capture of Mr. Sun";

The Chronicle of Higher Education: "In Memory of Lost Brain Cells";

The Decade Dance: "Mortal Love Watches the Dance";

The Harvard Review: "The Ballad of Jesse Helms";

Hubbub: "W. D. Studies the Spectra of Departure";

The Kenyon Review: "Snow Songs";

Light: "Hip Hop" and "Dumbbell Rhymes";

Michigan Quarterly Review: "Fox Trot: The Whisper, the Whistle and the Song" and "The Memory of Cock Robin Dwarfs W. D.";

The Nation: "Elena Ceauçescu's Bed";

North Dakota Review: "W. D. Sees Himself Animated," "The Forces of Love Re-assemble W. D." and "Cock Robin Escapes from the Alizarin of Evening";

Ploughshares: "Venus and the Lute Player";

Poetry: "As a Child, Sleepless" and "Autumn Variations";

Salmagundi: "Love Lamp," "Tunnel of Romance," "Mr. Evil Waltzes W. D.'s Thoughts Away from Cock Robin," "Mr. Evil Disguises Himself as Herself — with Murder in Her Heart for W. D.," "Human Torch" and "The Hall of Mirrors";

The Sewanee Review: "Pretexts" (originally titled "Versions") and "Birds Caught, Birds Flying";

The Southern Review: "Anniversary Verses for My Oldest Wife," "the girl outside your window," "In Flower," "An Envoi, Post-TURP." "An Old Flame," "Summer Sequence," "Spring Suite," "Apache: Miss Treavle Pursues W. D.," "Tango: W. D. Is Dwarfed by the Vision of Mr. Evil and Cock Robin," "Masquerada: Neither the Heat of the Mask nor the Point of the House Can Distract W. D. from Mr. Evil Disguised" and "Tap Dance: W. D. Escapes from Miss Treavle";

Tygers of Wrath: Poems of Hate, Anger and Invective (Edited by X. J. Kennedy, The University of Georgia Press): "A Teen-Ager";

William Ewert Broadsides: "Minuet in F##," "Mexican Hat Dance" and "From a Polish Cabaret";

The sequence herein entitled "The Midnight Carnival" was originally issued as a book entitled *W. D.'s Midnight Carnival* —with artwork by DeLoss McGraw — in a limited edition of handset poems and original etchings by Brighton Press and in a trade edition by ARTRA Publishing, Inc., in 1988.

Five of these poems, "To Shape a Song," "W. D. Sees Himself Animated," "Cock Robin Escapes from the Alizarin of Evening," "Tap Dance: W. D. Escapes from Miss Treavle" and "The Forces of Love Re-assemble W. D." were included in a limited, fine press volume entitled *To Shape a Song* — with artwork by DeLoss McGraw — and issued by the Nadja Press in 1988.

ABOUT THE AUTHOR

W. D. Snodgrass was born in Wilkinsburg, Pennsylvania, and educated at Geneva College and the University of Iowa. He has taught at the University of Rochester, Wayne State, Syracuse, Old Dominion, and the University of Delaware where he is currently Professor of English. He has received fellowships from the Guggenheim and Ingram Merrill foundations, the Academy of American Poets, the National Institute of Arts and Letters, and the National Endowment for the Arts. His first book, *Heart's Needle*, won the Pulitzer Prize for Poetry in 1960, and signalled the emergence of American confessional poetry. That work was followed by *After Experience* (1968), *The Fuhrer Bunker: A Cycle of Poems in Progress* (BOA Editions, 1977), and *Selected Poems* (1987). Mr. Snodgrass also has six volumes of translations to his credit, and *In Radical Pursuit*, a volume of literary criticism. *Each in His Season* is Mr. Snodgrass's eighth book of poetry.

BOA EDITIONS, LTD.
AMERICAN POETS CONTINUUM SERIES

Vol. 1   *The Führer Bunker: A Cycle of Poems in Progress*
         W. D. Snodgrass
Vol. 2   *She*
         M. L. Rosenthal
Vol. 3   *Living With Distance*
         Ralph J. Mills, Jr.
Vol. 4   *Not Just Any Death*
         Michael Waters
Vol. 5   *That Was Then: New and Selected Poems*
         Isabella Gardner
Vol. 6   *Things That Happen Where There Aren't Any People*
         William Stafford
Vol. 7   *The Bridge of Change: Poems 1974-1980*
         John Logan
Vol. 8   *Signatures*
         Joseph Stroud
Vol. 9   *People Live Here: Selected Poems 1949-1983*
         Louis Simpson
Vol. 10 *Yin*
         Carolyn Kizer
Vol. 11 *Duhamel: Ideas of Order in Little Canada*
         Bill Tremblay
Vol. 12 *Seeing It Was So*
         Anthony Piccione
Vol. 13 *Hyam Plutzik: The Collected Poems*
Vol. 14 *Good Woman: Poems and a Memoir 1969-1980*
         Lucille Clifton
Vol. 15 *Next: New Poems*
         Lucille Clifton
Vol. 16 *Roxa: Voices of the Culver Family*
         William B. Patrick
Vol. 17 *John Logan: The Collected Poems*
Vol. 18 *Isabella Gardner: The Collected Poems*
Vol. 19 *The Sunken Lightship*
         Peter Makuck
Vol. 20 *The City in Which I Love You*
         Li-Young Lee
Vol. 21 *Quilting: Poems 1987-1990*
         Lucille Clifton
Vol. 22 *John Logan: The Collected Fiction*
Vol. 23 *Shenandoah and Other Verse Plays*
         Delmore Schwartz